REAL TALK
MONEY TREE
SOIL & CROP

TENIKA JOWERS GOLDEN

ISBN: 978-1-965082-10-2

Publishing By: DemiCo National, LLC

www.DemiCoNational.com

TABLE OF CONTENTS

What's In Your Soil

Page 7

What's In Your Garden

Page 16

The Home Setting

Part 29

Don't Cheat Others

Page 34

Active & Passive Purpose

Page 39

Soil & Crop

Page 51

WHAT'S IN YOUR SOIL

In the early morning around 2AM, I was awakened by the Highest Power. As my eyes opened wide, He registered one thought in my spirit, REAL ESTATE. Then my place of work came to mind. He then asked me the question.

"What is the basis of real estate?"

"Soil." I replied, which is the foundation of most. Then He told me to research a soil inspector. I Googled, and *Soil Engineer* popped up. I began to read the importance of good soil when you're creating a foundation or an establishment. As I continued to read, I saw the differences between toxic and nutritional soil. Afterwards, He showed me the problems that many businesses have, which is the foundation of toxic soil.

The question at this point is, What's really in your soil? Before you build you have got to reach for the stars, which is the best. For example, in real estate, the best soil is Loam soil.

Loam soil is often considered one of the best types of soil for building, because it's balance of sand, silt, and clay. These contribute the right amount of:

1. Moisture, which loam absorbs and releases moisture at a steady rate, so it doesn't expand or shrink enough to damage the foundation.

2. Air circulation, which air can circulate well through loam, and it drains well.

3. Strength, which the loam is strong enough to support a foundation.

It's important to condition the soil before building a foundation to ensure there's nothing below ground that could shift over time. You should also filter out any un-decomposed material that might be in the loam.

So, bear with me, I'm trying to take you somewhere. Even though, this is literally how you start a build, this entire concept rolls over into building a business. Often, when businesses are built, they're put together in a rush by trying to fill a certain quota of people for startup; therefore, simply placing bodies in position, without truly examining if they really fit the criteria's needed.

I've known people to lie to relocate from one place to another after destroying their previous workplace. So, it's very important to have a proper research team, because that person will most definitely not be loam soil; I'm just saying. Also, while you're hiring, it's vital to make sure your employees are put in the right position. For example, in the basketball world, would you put your 6th man on the bench, that's only 5 feet tall, in to play center at the beginning of the game, to complete the starting five? I can assure you, that your answer is NO. Well, correct position placement is just as important in staff business.

You have people that are excellent behind the scenes and suck in the forefront. Even while separated, they must be strong to show concreteness for a successful business. Once this has taken place, to prevent deprivation in the foundation built, you cannot allow toxic traits to affect your loam.

Toxicity is the quality of being very harmful or unpleasant in a pervasive or insidious way. This is real and it can destroy your place of business. These are some things that add toxicity to your soil (the foundation of business):

1. Pervasiveness is the quality of spreading widely or being present through every part of something being pervasive of an unwelcome influence.

2. Being insidious, which is proceeding in a gradual, subtle way, but with harmful effects.

3. Micromanaging is when someone tries to control every part of a situation, project, etc., even including the small details, in

a way that may not be necessary, and may not give enough responsibility to other employees.

4. The lack of communication, with zero people skills, will affect the entire establishment.

5. The lack of official improvement in self-leadership.

6. The overall lack in setting an example.

So, these issues need to be avoided for the credential's sake of your company. Now this is a brief writing on the foundation of what's in the business's soil. The soil is so important, because you should always remember, it doesn't matter what the building looks like to remain there. I've seen a beautiful mansion destroyed, because the soil was toxic. The toxic soil caused cracks in the ceiling, the floors, and foundation to sink. This is why people will live and work in a small compact building; to be surrounded by a solid foundation with longevity.

REAL TALK

It is better to not have a team, than to have the wrong team on the ground level of your business. Your foundation is everything, and you have to trust that everyone on the ground level shares the same core company values. Failure to do so will always result in disaster.

Use the following lines to journal "What's In Your Soil".

_____

_____

_____

_____

_____

_____

_____

_____

WHAT'S IN YOUR GARDEN

What you have in your garden, is the bloodline to the core of the business. To be able to produce good fruit and products, you must take care of the soil; which should be fertilized properly. This healthy soil contains the handpicked, qualified, chain of commands, in top managements, on down to the basic employees. Once provided with the proper nourishment in the soil, you can then drop the seeds for them to grow greatly. If a company can give customers the desires and wants that they are looking for, then surely it can give them what they need.

So, that being addressed, we have to go back to the soil, and how the seeds are nourished. As a company, as a whole, it's a lot that comes with nourishing the seeds (employees). The minerals have to be so good that you can tell that the babies are developing properly. You have to consider the workplace or your career, like it's a baby you're developing in your garden.

Babies develop in great conditions when taken care of, and when spoken to properly from the womb, in conception, and then even after birth. Sometimes, situations can occur that make the employee feel inadequate due to multiple things going wrong. That's when you teach them to calm down and breathe; then focus on the problems one at a time. This builds trust.

If you don't want abnormalities or disfunction, then you must act like you want to actually take care of the needs of the child, fruit, or whatever the products are. Show empathy and sympathize when needed. So, eliminate soil pollution that will affect fertility, and jeopardize security for the upcoming business. Beware not to give the employees empty promises, too. Basically, just put your money where your mouth is. It's also important that, as the teams are being developed throughout daily processes, teach them how to build as individuals personally, and enhance the job requirements.

This starts with the mind, because for stability to take place, it's always a mind over matter thing. I say that because, everyday isn't going to be a breeze, with peaches, and cream. That's why it's important to plant as many palm trees in your garden as possible. You should have employees that can handle the storms of business.

Palm trees are flexible, strong, and can stand the test of times. You can build them by speaking life to the employees, training, and teaching the *do's and don'ts* of the company:

- Become trustworthy, so you can be trusted

- Encourage teamwork, learning

- Maintain a positive environment

- Give the proper tools that's needed to be of great success

- Recognize and acknowledge work ethics and accomplishments

- Support valuable new ideas

- Share your vision

- Get other opinions for betterment

- Discuss advance opportunities

- Be transparent

- Celebrate milestones

- Be thankful for your employees

- Get to know them

- Set an example

This will keep employee retainment in the company, because you're taking care of your crop. Then your crop will take care of you by producing the best quality products and loyalty. Now if your company is failing, then I can give you examples of what might be the problem there, and how the issues may be destroying your crop. This is an often-asked question and is puzzling to the employer. How can 1000 seeds be planted and only 100 quality products produced?

If this is your situation, then something is surely causing the default. When your garden isn't nourished, you have to make sure that if anything is stunting the growth of the crop, then those weeds need to be eliminated. Your company is now experiencing depletion, which is the reduction in the number or quantity of the company, resulting in deprivation.

Deprivation is the degree to which an individual or an area is deprived of services due to the lack of retainment. So, if you're lacking in staffing, then some changes have to be made. I've seen leaders expect an employee to become superman & superwoman, squeezing blood out of a turnip, and without having a guideline in place to even teach them how to do so. Often times, an employee figures out how to do multiple jobs at one time successfully and still don't get the recognition deserved, which is another crop killer.

Micromanaging, is another fatal action for business. Everyone feels entirely suffocated, because leadership doesn't give them the opportunity to expedite in the knowledge learned, which also stunts their growth. Ongoingly, the biggest weed in the garden will be from this type of management; clearly representing poor people's skills and ending in the lack of retaining employees.

If a leader does not present themselves respectfully, then it can destroy the entire garden. Communication is key, and the tones are a huge factor. Body language plays a part in setting the atmosphere. So, when communication skills are dysfunctional, it makes everyone question your position and character.

If you didn't know, it's a form of bullying. The employees scratch their heads and wonder if you've been bullied in the past and not healed from the trauma.

This action might appear that you are seeking attention, by acting out or throwing a tantrum. If that's what you enjoy doing, then clap your hand to your defeat, and pull out some plant killer, and spray it everywhere, because your message is 'I don't care about you.' If your vibe is negative, it disrupts the spirits of whoever you're relating to. Now, you have nasty attitudes floating around, because of the way you presented yourself.

This causes an electrical effect of negativity, triggering throughout the garden during the entire day, and the morale drops from 100 to 0 quickly. The hope and desire to work starts to deteriorate. Employees then start to analyze how miserable they are. The smiles begin to fade and their attendance does too. And before you know it, they become unbothered about work.

This is a side effect of what toxic soil looks like; when weeds are fertilized instead of the actual crop. So, as a leader, do you want to be talked about as it pertains to how immature you are throughout the entire shift? Even after employees clock out, they're still talking about how unprofessional you are while going to their vehicles to go home.

After getting in the car, they call their besties or homeboy to complain about going on *Indeed,* and other hiring sites, to send resumes, to search for another job. And to top it all off, you are the pillow talk to their mates; which the fact upsets the significant other encouraging them to seek other employment. So, this domino effect destroys the foundation (soil) and the garden (crop), the employees developing, and the products being built and sold. In the end game, respect is lost and you're not retaining staff. Real talk; with results of a Ghost House, no employees, and an unsuccessful business. I honestly think of the old saying, 'one bad apple can spoil the whole bunch,' when I see a business flop like this. That's why, your actions and the way you conduct yourself is very important. This should be a constant reminder, that you will receive whatever you have delivered. So, step back and take a good look at the workplace, or should I state, observe what's really in your garden. Let's face it, each individual needs to examine whatever issues needs to be addressed by self-evaluation.

If you can see the issues that are existing, and the weeds that are killing the crop, then ask yourself if you are contributing to the problem. If your answer is yes, then you need some mirror-time, work on self-improvement, personal development, take accountability, address with action to change whatever you need to work on.

Because, when you're in leadership or any role at a corporation, you must look at the entire company and not focus on yourself. Always remember, what you do can affect business as a whole and the atmosphere. So, in the workplace, everyone has to grasp the concept of respecting your peers and putting that into action. That's truly how you win personally and in business, but if you choose otherwise and become disrespectful, you'll lose EVERY TIME.

Regardless of how this is received, self-conflicts are like poison. Self-conflict is a type of conflict that takes place inside a character's (your) mind. Man vs Self, which conflict involves the main character's inner struggle with self-doubts. However, it's never too late to fix the you that's broken with positive collaboration and get evolved. You will eventually find yourself feeling uplifted, because you decided not to be the one Bad Apple planted in your business garden. Regroup, relax, relate, release and regrow your garden by eliminating the weeds. Then, your crop has room to expand and produce all of the supply for the customer's demand.

REAL TALK

I cannot explain the importance of minding your madness enough. There's no other way to call it. Listen, we are living in the most stressful and anxious time in modern history, and no one has the temperament we all had ten or even twenty years ago. So, what does that mean? It means, treating people like you don't want to end up on the six o'clock news! Talk to people like you have sense. When you bully, humiliate, insult, and play yo-yo with someone's job, and place they rely on to provide for their family, you are playing with fire! I am never an advocate for violence of any sort, but we're too old to be acting as if we don't know the world we live in. Don't be the final straw that pushes someone over the edge; putting your life, safety, and that of others at risk, simply because you refuse to show respect to someone.

Use the following lines to journal "What's In Your garden".

THE HOME SETTING

I would like to thank you for taking the time out of your day to embrace this book. Yes, this is a business book. But, what good is it to excel in the workplace, but you're miserable at home? Throughout the read, you discovered the foundation and how you take care of your crop. This is a must in creating a dynamic business.

Well, it's a known fact that people have problems providing the same behaviors at home. Why not put on your cape and spread the goodies and this information there as well. Let's face it, the happier you are as a whole, the better you can produce in your place of business. As a matter of fact, I dare you to take action. Sit back and then watch the development. Whether you're in a relationship with your mate, or even with your children, it's so important to have understanding. Communication is always key.

While the communication is becoming so golden, add a hint of speaking life into one another. That too can enhance encouragement.

When you've established this type of environment in your home, then no matter how life delivers, the family can stand through trying times; having a better chance of remaining positive throughout all situations. I'm talking about a whole pot of greatness being cooked on the stove.

REAL TALK

So, when you gather your bowls and serve this nutritious meal to you and your family, it will create power from inside out. The family will then be built on stability, which motivates them all to pursue their goals and dreams. All of this makes your foundation solid, not toxic, which provides capabilities for everyone in your home to produce and grow with great health and wealth.

Now the glue is in the home, it keeps the family sealed together with strength and longevity. Since that's all in a nutshell, go live your best life and be GREAT.

Use the following lines to journal any closing notes.

DON'T CHEAT OTHERS

You have joined me on this journey to expand our minds as it pertains to our unhealthy habits that often sabotage our likelihood of success as employees or as entrepreneurs. Here's the truth. It all starts with a solid foundation, and now that we've studied the importance of that foundation, I have to stress the importance of doing unto others as you would have them do unto you. Don't cheat others.

Have you heard the story of the farmer and the baker? Once, there was a farmer who sold a pound of butter to a baker. One day, the baker decided to weigh the butter to see if he was getting the right amount. The baker confirmed that he was receiving less than a pound of butter from the farmer. He was angry about this, so, he took the farmer to court. The judge asked the farmer if he was using any measure to weigh the butter. The farmer replied, "Your Honor, I am primitive. I don't have a proper measure, but I do have a scale." The judge asked, "Then how do you weigh the butter?" The farmer replied, "Your Honor, long before the baker started buying butter from me, I have been buying a pound of a loaf of bread from him. Every day, when the baker brings the bread, I put it on the scale and give him the same weight in butter. If anyone is to be blamed, it is the baker." Remember this, my friends, in life and in business; you get what you give. Don't try to cheat others.

Just as the farmer gave the baker the same weight in butter as the bread he received, in life, we get what we give. When we act with honesty, fairness, and generosity, we create a cycle that benefits both ourselves and others. Attempting to cheat or deceive others leads to negative consequences, as seen in the case of the baker's attempt to cheat the farmer.

REAL TALK

Here is the truth. When you cheat others, you cheat yourself out of the purpose God has planned for you. Trust me when I say this. There is no dollar amount worth the favor of God.

Use the following lines to journal financial code of ethics.

ACTIVE AND PASSIVE PURPOSE

This chapter is a total bonus from the mouth of a millionaire. It's a little deep and a lot to digest, but it's important for your financial journey. So, are you ready to eat the crop? Here it is:

This is the cheat code every millionaire practices. This cheat code will also help alleviate stress if you are an employee or entrepreneur. The ability to not rely solely on one source of income, is not only a chance of living a much more stress-free life, it's also a chance of building unmeasurable wealth. Let's discuss Passive and Active income strategies.

Passive income sounds magical, but is it really better than active income? And what exactly is the difference between active and passive income? We'll define both and show you the differences, including which types of income qualify as active and which are passive. Both incomes are required throughout your lifetime but combining the power of both can help you reach financial independence much faster.

Active Income vs. Passive Income: What's the Difference?

While both types of income require some sort of work, they are fundamentally different.

Active income requires you to materially participate in a work-related activity to earn money, while passive income comes from owning income-producing assets. You typically need to earn active income first to generate the funds needed to invest in passive income assets.

What Is Active Income?

Active income is the process of working for money and includes things like wages, salary, tips, commissions, freelance income, side hustle income, and other work-related income. In most cases, you are trading your time for money.

What Is Passive Income?

Passive income includes earning income without being required to participate in a work-related activity. This includes income from sources like investments, dividends, real estate rentals, business ownership, online businesses, courses, downloadable content, existing YouTube channel, website display ads, affiliate marketing and more.

Here are a few examples of ways to earn active income:

- Your job. The most common way to earn active income is through your job. Whether you are paid hourly or an annual salary, you show up to work, do your job and get paid.
- Your business. If you own a business and haven't hired an operator and management team to handle all of the day-to-day tasks, then you are earning active income. If you are

handling any aspect of the business operations, such as sales calls or providing a service, this is considered active.

- Freelance work. Freelance work is considered active income, as you are providing a service for pay. This might include freelance video editing, writing, software development, legal consulting or any other type of contract work.

- Gig economy work. Jobs like driving for Uber or Doordash, pet sitting, house-sitting or other gig economy jobs qualify as active income.

Here are a few examples of ways to earn passive income:

- Traditional investments. Investing in the stock market puts your money to work, and you can earn interest, dividends and capital gains from your investments. This is a completely passive activity, allowing you to earn money without doing anything more than investing your funds.

- Bank Interest. When you deposit your money in a savings account, you can earn passive income based on the account interest rate. Even better, finding a high-yield savings account will pay you a higher rate without having to lift a finger. This is truly passive income.

- Dividends. Whether you earn dividends from investing in a stock or bond, or if it's from a business you own, dividends are paid without you needing to work for them. For traditional investments, these are typically paid out on a quarterly or monthly basis.

- Rental real estate. Rental real estate is one of the best ways to earn passive income, though you do need to invest funds (and time) into getting the property rented and managed. While real estate may require some of your time, once it is rented out and you hire a management team, it can be nearly 100% hands-off income.

- Online income. While building an online business takes a lot of time, once you have established a system for generating leads and income, you can automate a lot of the process. For larger online businesses, hiring an operations and leadership team can help you simply collect income without participating in the business.

Active income and passive income are treated differently by the IRS. While active income is typically taxed at your normal income tax rates (and taken from your paycheck directly), passive income taxes can vary, depending on how the income is generated.

Passive income can be taxed at a lower rate, at your regular income tax rate or even at a higher rate, depending on how it is earned. Because investment rules vary widely, it's best to work with a licensed tax professional when managing taxes for passive income streams.

How Combining Active and Passive Income Helps You Earn More:

While active income is the most common way to earn money, passive income helps you earn money without putting in any extra work.

But what if you did both? Focusing on increasing your active income can help you save more money each month. You can then use the savings to invest in income-generating assets such as investments, businesses, rental real estate or even just depositing it into a high-interest account.

The more you invest into passive income, the higher your annual earnings will be. Eventually, your investments might outpace your active income, and then you will become financially independent, able to live on your passive income alone.

Here's how combining your active and passive income can raise your overall income:

- Hourly Rate: $20 an hour
- Annual Income: $41,600

- Invest 15% of income: $6,240

Over the next five years, if your investments provide an average return of 8% per year, you'll end up with over $45,000. These funds earning 8% per year can now earn $3,600 in the next year. That's the equivalent of giving yourself a $1.73 raise, without doing any extra work.

REAL TALK

Both active and passive income are necessary to increase your income and eventually be able to retire. You will most likely start with active income, working for a company, and then slowly transition to passive income over time.

Eventually, you will retire and live 100% on passive income, but you need to start investing in income-producing assets today, to build your passive income. This is a long-term strategy — and one that's required to have a comfortable retirement.

Use the following lines to journal your ACTIVE and PASSIVE income prospects.

_____

_____

_____

_____

_____

_____

_____

_____

_____

_____

_____

_____

_____

SOIL & CROP

The Closing

S   STARTING

O   ON

I   IMPRENETRABLE

L   LOVE

Where you start in life, will always determine not only where you end, but how you end. Because I know, that when all is said and done, we all seek to receive love, it is important that we start with love. Start your business, dream, career, or pursuit of greater with the highest intent to be a vessel of love. While you may not be able to walk around your place of work just telling everyone how much you love them, you can show them love. You can show others just how you love yourself, and others, by how you treat them. Build with love and always be mindful to never plant anything that will contradict your ability to show love to self and others.

C   CREATING

R   REALITY

O   ON

P   PURPOSE

In life, there are always two realities at hand; the reality we accept and the reality we deny. I cannot explain how important it is for you to be intentional about creating the reality you wish to experience at your place of business. The last thing that you want to occur is for you to experience one reality, while all of your employees or team members experience an entirely different reality. As long as you share the same reality that they share, they will always feel seen, understood, and offer patience. This concept transcends the professional space of life, but can be applied to our home life as well. Be intentional about creating the reality you desire those you love to experience- a space where everyone feels safe, respected, and valued. This is your crop. This is your chance. Real Talk.

THE END